75+

College

Tips

(Your parents won't tell you about!)

By

Melissa 'the Great'

2013

Printed in the United States of America

First Edition – 2013

Cover Design: Triplicity Publishing, LLC

Interior Design: Triplicity Publishing, LLC

Dedication

This book is dedicated to all of the naive college newbie's out there that were not allowed out of the house as teens.

75+ Tips

When I started college, the University mailed me a checklist. Remembering to bring a toothbrush is dandy, but what about a warning, or tips for my first year that were actually useful and not a list of suggestions? So, I decided to write one myself, not just for me, because I have long since graduated, but for the future generations. If you are reading this and thinking to yourself, "Are these tips taken from actual events?" Yes, and that knowledge will now help you! So, sit back, relax, and read my tips that are in no particular order...and by the way, You Are Welcome!

1. College is NOW, and high school was then. It doesn't matter what category you did fit into, this is a new start.
2. So, you have never been away from home or your parents. You are nervous and scared.Get over it. There are thousands of students just like you who are learning to be on their own too.
3. Always wear sandals in the dorm showers, otherwise you might get foot fungus and that is just gross.
4. Learn how to do your own laundry before going to college. Ask your parents and take notes, or ask the internet.
5. Adapt to your surroundings. Know your way around the campus and city. Before school starts, navigate

through the area. You will look way less like a "newbie" without a map in your hands, stumbling around campus.

6. There are bicyclists, skateboarders, and of course walkers on campus...do not be the weirdo in spandex and wrist pads on rollerblades.

7. Do not sign-up for credit cards. Just because they entice you with free stuff, like t-shirts, I-pods, etc., in the long run you will end up in debt. Let's face it, you don't have a job yet, and don't you actually want to be able to finance things in your future when you do have a job?

8. Keep your life private on social network sites and maintain account settings with total privacy between you and your family and some friends. You do not have to 'friend' everyone you meet. Eventually, when you are older and applying for jobs or internships, companies will Google you.

9. Once you turn eighteen, there will be a sign-up table to register to vote. Then you will be eligible for Jury Duty. If you do not want to attend you can send the card back saying you are in college. If you do want to attend Jury Duty, then the professors have to let you miss class.

10. The first year requirement classes that have more than 50 students, means that the professors do not take attendance and do not care whether or not you

attend (especially because you have bought their book so they get paid either way). Therefore, when you skip a class you are only hurting yourself. It is not high school, professors do not keep track of you.

11. If you are struggling with a class, do not be afraid of acquiring a tutor. Again, professors will not tutor you and they do not spend one on one time with each student. Look around campus bulletins, there are postings for tutors everywhere.

12. You are ultimately paying for college. Scholarships can be taken away for bad grades and eventually, once you graduate, you have to pay back student loans. So, the moral is go to class and take advantage of everything the University has to offer.

13. If you were the class clown in high school, do not take your outbursts into a college classroom. The outcome will not be funny and you will find yourself hearing crickets after a comment that you find hilarious.

14. Now that technology rules our lives, cell phones are a common device. Again you are paying for your classes, so turn your cell phone off and pay attention. In most cases, if it goes off in class the professor will tell you to leave or embarrass the crap out of you and your stupid ringtone.

15. If you do not have a vehicle, or the campus does not allow it your freshman year, make a friend with

someone that does have transportation. This will come in handy for weekend trips home, and most importantly, groceries.

16. Never shop for food hungry! You will save more money this way.

17. Familiarize yourself with the grocery store. Find what you like and stick to a list you make each week. The more you impulse buy for food, the more weight you will gain.

18. If you have the dining paid for the first year, like most colleges offer, eat breakfast, lunch, and dinner at the campus food sites you or your parents are paying for. Otherwise, you are wasting money. But eat healthy, do not eat just the pizza.

19. A rotating sign holder on the side of the road is not a good job. I would not trust cars driving by with your life. Plus, it is not a good way to ask someone out on a date.

20. If you have never experienced alcohol, do not binge drink. Gradually move into drinking liquor. Start with one or two. Learn your tolerance. Most young adults that have never had a drink will indulge too much and flunk out of college the first semester.

21. Parties and drinking are for letting go when you are done with school work. Do not let the party life fool you. If you see some of your friends always going out, but maintaining good grades, it does not mean

you can, they might have an easy major like elementary education.

22. If you do decide to go out frequently, look for specials. A lot of restaurants and bars have different specials each night of the week. This is where you will meet people and it will save you money.

23. Foam parties sound fun but are disgusting. Do you really want to walk around with wet underwear all night? If you do go to a foam party as a girl, go in a group, hold hands, and leave as a group.

24. Male or female, whether at a bar, or especially a house party, watch closely to your drinks being poured. Do not take a drink blind, you do not know if drugs were snuck in! And guys, females are just as likely to spike a drink as a man, they like sex too!

25. If hunch punch is at a party with fruit, eat the fruit. If you are going to partake in drinking, at least you are eating too. (See Hunch Punch recipe)

26. If there are only brownies at a party and no other food, you are going to get high. Use common sense; Lots of alcohol and no food, but only brownies equals pot brownies.

27. If someone at a party offers you a mushroom from a freezer in a Ziploc bag, do not eat it. Walk away. These are not garden fresh vegetables, these will make you hallucinate and end up naked in a random courtyard, surrounded by imaginary animals.

28. Keep your college ID, because after college, even 10 years later, you can use it to get discounts. If your hair starts to gray, color it.
29. Red solo cups are obvious. Coke bottles, gas station Styrofoam cups, and coffee cups can act as a decoy for when you have alcohol.
30. Mingle. Make friends. If you aren't studying do not be afraid to walk around campus and meet people. Every campus has a union and it is a great place to hang out.
31. If you take a bicycle to college, make sure you familiarize yourself with bicycle safety rules before you ride it on campus. Campus police make their money off of bicycle tickets. Get a light, obey the speed limit, and please don't try to be cool and ride with no hands, you will get pulled over!
32. If you are not a born again Christian, do not room with a religious student. Most likely he/she will have parents that show up, unannounced, at any 'fun' moment and ruin your night. You do not want a sixty year old woman speaking to you in tongues while you are wearing a towel.
33. If you end up having a religious roommate, nonchalantly leave a playgirl or playboy on their bed, it could change their life and yours! For the better.

34. Go to Football games and try to go to other school sporting events as well. Tailgate. (See How to Tailgate)

35. Road trips. Road trips. Road trips. Make new friends and tour cities outside of the college. Take lots of pictures and stop at odd stores and restaurants. Buy stupid hats and take more pictures. Some of your best memories can be from a spontaneous road trip.

36. If your apartment neighbors have an annoying cat that follows you into the apartment, shave it down the middle, add a bell to its collar, and put it outside. You will never see that cat again.

37. How can you be different when throwing a party? Do not be basic. Most people just throw a party. Make yours themed. For example, 80's music and dress, Groundhog Day, and my personal favorite April Fool's Day.

38. Go halfzies with your neighbors on a keg to keep for adjoining parties. It will save you money in the long run.

39. Invest in a karaoke machine. When annoying guests will not leave your place, turn it on. This always works. They will disappear.

40. If you are making flaming drinks or doing a 'fireball' at a party, do not spill alcohol on your arms or clothes, you will be set on fire!

41. Do not overload your fridge with food. Eventually, you will need a lot of room for Jello shots. (See Jello Shots recipe)

42. When you throw a party, be prepared for the group you invited to multiply by 50% or more. You will not know these people. Lock up all jewelry and very important belongings, like sunglasses. At one point, bust out the karaoke machine. It does not matter if you live in a gated complex, the people will come.

43. Drinking games are a great way to break the ice at parties. (See Drinking games)

44. If you trip on air while walking through campus look forward with your head held high. Never walk with your head down. Show confidence. Plus, you never know if a damn skateboarder is about to run you down.

45. If you are wearing earphones while walking through campus you might want to leave one ear bud out. Besides the fact that you will not hear a bike rider ringing their bell before they slam into you, you might miss a girl/boy saying your name and this could be your Friday night date.

46. Do not have the volume turned to the highest level if you are wearing headphones. You will get hit by a damn skateboarder and you will go deaf in one ear.

47. Do not pledge to a frat or sorority unless your parents were members and you have to, or you want

to have your entire college career planned out, days, nights, and weekends. There are other clubs and things to experience on campus for all kinds of people, even wizards.

48. Stay away from the Hare Krishnas on campus and in front of the stadium on game days. Yes, their tambourines will draw you in and so will the smell of their free stew, but it will only give you the runs and it will happen while you are sitting in class.

49. Do not become a follower. Who cares if you meet a hot looking vegetarian who wants you to protest with them at a rally. You will get bacon thrown on you, and if this does happen bring a Ziploc. Bacon isn't cheap.

50. Have well rounded friends: a couple of partiers, a laid back person, an organizer, and a nerd.

51. Make friends in different majors. They can help you with the boring requirement classes and after college it is always good to know a pharmacist or a lawyer.

52. Make at least one nerd friend. They can help tutor your group of friends and do so because you let them hang out. Plus, they will always be the designated driver. Also, when you are older, you won't care if they are nerdy when their invention and ideas help make you money!

53. I do not care what you think; Wal-Mart in the middle of the night is cool. Especially, chilling on a

hammock, eating Oreos, and people watching; just make sure you pay for the Oreos.

54. Walk around RVs on football mornings. Alumni are the best tailgaters and will always give students food. Be prepared and bring a paper plate and plastic fork.

55. Do not play video games all of the time, you will miss out on real life. Instead of video games, get a group together for laser tag or kickball in the park.

56. Pay your parking tickets right away or at the end of the semester you will be standing in a very long line. If this happens bring refreshments.

57. There is always great music to be found any day of the week around a college city. Go to small venues or big venues and hear bands. You never know if one day you will say, "I saw them before they were famous."

58. Beer goggles are truth, not a myth. Most likely if you pick someone up at a bar, the next morning you will know what regret means. Take a very, very hot shower.

59. Know the mascot of your school and its nickname.

60. Know the actual colors of your school.

61. Never wear a rival college's school colors or their actual attire. Do not be that student that likes another school and says, "I am just here for the academics."

62. If you do not like sports, do not go to the games. If you pretend and later tell your friends you are bored, you might as well leave and make new friends at the community college down the street.

63. If you do not know how to cook basic meals, use the internet. You cannot survive four years, or 7 if you are a smart med student, on McDonalds or ramen noodles. Find a roommate that likes to cook, better yet, find a roommate that wants to be a chef!

64. Do not get engaged. Do not get married. You will meet 10 different soul mates over the course of your college career.

65. Do not live with your parents if you reside in the same town as your college. You will experience nothing.

66. Do not rent movies or sell baked goods out of your dorm room, unless you keep it underground, and you are friends with the RA. You will get caught, and it is illegal without a permit. But if you do it right, it can be a lucrative business.

67. Do not purchase or have anything that requires responsibility; such as an animal or child. You will forget to take it out and feed it.

68. Allow your parents to visit. They will buy you food for a month, and for some, who have liberal parents, alcohol.

69. In college, most likely you are still on your parent's health insurance. If you get sick, take advantage and go to the doctor. Once you are out of school and on your own in charge of your benefits, you will be glad you "learned the ropes."

70. Do not schedule early classes unless you are a morning person. But, it is the best time to shower if you are living in the dorms.

71. The 'Freshman 10' is more likely going to be the 'Freshman 20.' Watch your beer and pizza intake. Substitute flatbread, add some vegetables to the pizza, and drink light beer.

72. Take advantage of the campus gym and make a routine. After college you will thank yourself (and me).

73. Beer is not water. Remember, hydrate, you do not want to scare your parents to death with a call from the hospital because you have alcohol poisoning.

74. Take good notes, because you never know if the hot guy/girl in the class wants to hang out at your place and borrow your notes. Make sure you do not drool on your notebook while sleeping.

75. Do not carry over your high school relationship to college; even if you go to the same University. If it is meant to be, you will get back together after school. Agree to be friends.

76. Move out of the dorms after your freshman year. Find an apartment with roommates you know and that are reliable. Your partying friends are fun, but do not make good roommates.

77. If your roommate's bf/gf is eating food off of the floor, then he/she is probably mentally unstable and you both should run.

78. Do not feed bread to the two ducks at the retention pond by your place. The entire flock will appear at your doorstep and cause a traffic jam. They will find you.

79. A scooter is not the best transportation, especially when it rains a lot and gets cold. If you do get a scooter, at least wear snoopy goggles and walk with a strut.

80. Coffee is your friend. Learn to like it. You do not want to turn to drugs or a dependence on red bull to study. Coffee is much safer.

81. Study groups go nowhere, they turn into gossip sessions. Now is the chance to rely on your nerd friend as a study partner.

82. STDs and Crabs are real! If you do not want to go through life scratching it, protect it!

83. No time to iron? Use a dryer with two bounce sheets, still works for me. Or use Dryel, so you do not have to dry clean.

84. Spring Break is a time of letting go. Do not go home for break. The whole point of Spring Break is to travel to a new place making incredible memories to tell your grandchildren one day.

85. Do not get so crazy on Spring Break that you get kicked out of college, thrown in jail, and worse, pregnant (if you are a girl) or have an illegitimate baby (if you are a boy).

86. If you take summer classes, it is always good to have a summer job as well. Movie theaters are great because usually as part time help, you do not have to work many hours and you get to see movies for free. Also, coffee shops are a perk, because again, free coffee!

87. School loans take a lengthy time to payback, if you can pay the interest while in school this will help lower your payments when college is complete.

88. You only get one chance at life, don't drink too much and drive and don't text and drive; that is what your designated driver is for!

Drinking Games

1. Quarters- This game can be played with any number of players, but it is best with 3-6. Each player has a drink and a mug or cup that is empty for the quarters. Decide on how much is consumed before the game starts. Everyone sits around a table, hard wood tables are best. Never use glass tables. Spin the quarter on the table, when it stops, the person it's closest to starts first. The first player tries to bounce a quarter off the table into a cup. If the quarter goes into the cup, the player chooses someone at the table to drink. Then, play continues. The player's turn is over when the quarter does not make it into a cup. A variation that is fast and exciting is having 2 quarters going simultaneously with two mugs, if the opposite player gets their quarter into the mug before the other player can get their quarter into a mug, the losing player must drink This is usually done with shots.

2. Flip Cup- You will need 2 teams divided into 4-5 players, and each with a solo cup filled with beer or a shot. Start at the end of a table. The first players on each team empties their cups by drinking. Then they start flipping the cup from the edge of the table with their fingers. Once the cup flips over

upside down the next player on their team goes. Obviously, the team that finishes first wins.

3. Beer Pong- You will need 12 solo cups full of beer and one ping pong ball. On one long table divide 6 cups on each side like bowling pins. Each team is on opposite ends of the table. Each turn you must throw the ball into the opposing team's cups. If it lands in a cup that team must drink the beer immediately. Then reposition the cups so they are close to each other again. The losing team is left with no cups. Once the game is over the losing team must drink the winning team's beer.

4. Bullshit- You will need a deck of cards. This is best with 3 or more players. One player deals out the entire deck. The first player to go starts with an Ace, and they lay face down the amount they have and say so out loud, "2 Aces," the next player then has 2's, then the next 3's, and so on to King then repeat the process. The point of the game is to bluff on how many cards you are laying face down. If someone does not believe you, they can call Bullshit. If they are right and you bluffed then you take the pile of cards in the middle. If they are wrong and you told the truth, then they take the pile. The winner is the player that gets rid of their cards first. To add drinking, add a shot to the player

that is called on their bluff or the player that loses the call.

5. Chandeliers-Start by setting up one large glass of beer in the middle of the table. Then each player sets up a cup in front of that glass where they are standing also filled with beer. The point of the game is to bounce a quarter into another player's cup. If you bounce a quarter in the middle glass then you choose who drinks that whole glass or in some groups everyone, but you must drink the entire cups and you still pick a player to drink the middle cup. Refill and start over.

Melissa 'the Great'

Drink Recipes

1. Hunch Punch Recipe: Use a clean cooler, the bigger the party, the bigger the cooler. Add one bottle of vodka, one bottle of clear rum, one bottle of fruit punch. Then add tons of chopped fruit; watermelon, strawberries, honey dew, cantaloupe, and grapes. Then finish with lots of ice. (some people like to add Sprite)

2. Jello Shots: You will need to buy little plastic cups found in the paper goods aisle at stores, and boxes of different flavored Jello. Boil one cup of water, once boiling add to bowl with a packet of Jello. Stir well, then add one cup of desired liquor. Add a few cubes of ice to help with heat. Then start pouring into plastic cups (the ice will help not melt these cups). It is best to use trays like baking sheets so they are easy to carry and place into the fridge. To be creative try matching liquor with Jello flavors. For example, tequila pairs well with lime, and vodka with strawberry or cherry. Rum is a tough one, but practice has shown it pairs well with raspberry and orange.

3. Easy Margaritas- If you do not have bartending tools, get one solo cup and a regular glass. Fill glass with ice, pour tequila (a bartender's trick is to count to 3, this is a shot), then add margarita mix (easily found

in any store near the wine section with other mixes). Put the solo cup over glass and shake from side to side. This technique helps mix the concoction together. For parties mix in a large pitcher. These can be bought cheap if they are plastic. If you're drinking out of the pitcher, find long straws.

4. Long Island Ice Tea- This drink can be done many ways, but my way, is any clear liquor that is found, add a shot of each in a tall glass filled with ice. Then add a splash of Coke (or Pepsi), and a squeeze of lemon. The best way to keep lemon juice on hand, is to buy the juice that is in a shape of a lemon in the fruits and vegetable section of the grocery store. Real lemons eventually go bad, this will last awhile.

5. Buttery Nipple-This can be a shot. In a shot glass add 1 ½ ounce of butterscotch liqueur and ½ ounce of Irish cream liqueur.

6. Blow Job- Make a buttery nipple and add whip cream to the top. Then, drink it with no hands.

7. Flaming Dr. Pepper- Take a shot glass and first pour 1 ½ of amaretto liqueur, then slowly pour 151 alcohol on top, to do not mix, they are meant to be layered. Then with a lighter (I use a long grill lighter) light the shot, it will then flame from the 151. Drop the shot into a glass filled halfway with beer. Immediately drink!

8. Fireball-This shot is the most dangerous, please be careful, the hair on my knuckles is gone from many fireballs gone wrong. Only perform this shot outside. Basically, you put a shot of 151 in your mouth, and in one hand have a lighter lit (I recommend a grill lighter for safety) and spit the 151 onto the fire and away from anything flammable, like your hair!

These are my most used recipes when I was in college. They are easy and simple and you do not have to be an established bartender to make them. If you want more recipes, I suggest you search the internet.

Tailgating

If you are going to an away game, then you should prepare for the pre-party fun. Tailgating is an art to some and it is something I have mastered over the years. You will always forget something, but the good news is that there are tons of tailgaters surrounding you and even rival school students or alumni will help out if you need to light a grill or forgot paper towels.

Where are you going? Is it going to be cold, hot, or raining? Check the weather the night before. Bring ponchos or a rain jacket. An extra pair of sandals or sneakers is good for the ride home if it has been raining all day. Plan to arrive early. The early tailgaters get the best parking. You want to have your vehicle parked so that you are able to put the tail gate down or trunk up facing other tailgaters. It is more fun to socialize once the funs starts. Turn off your interior car or truck lights, this way your battery doesn't die, and you will be able to keep the radio on, or hook-up an I-pod.

How many people are coming with you? Everyone should bring a chair. The best tailgating chairs have your team logo and drink holders. Bring solo cups for drinking games, and drink Cozies also with your team logo. Do not forget paper towels, plastic ware for eating, and paper or throw away plastic plates. Decide what you are going to eat. If you are a grill master, find a small hibachi grill at a sport's store or hardware store. I suggest a one-use grill that you can find at a grocery store in the charcoal aisle. It comes with its own charcoal and make shift grill. When you are done it is easily thrown away in a trash can. Bring one trash bag. When the game is about to start, you can clean up, and walk that bag to a trash can that all parking lots are equipped with.

Do not forget the munchies; chips, pickles, fruit, dips, etc. If you are drinking and are under age, be careful, most tailgating lots now have security checking ID's. If you see an opposing team, do not badger them, do not start a fight. Most couples nowadays have stories about meeting their spouses at different colleges. Why do you think they have license plates that say, "A house divided," then two separate schools on the plate? Why not invite them to play a game of beer pong. The bean bag toss game is fun, and can usually be found at most toy stores or sport's stores.

Once you get older and start tailgating at more events, like concerts, NFL, Baseball, etc., you will find ways to improve your experience. I learned a long time ago if it is going to rain or is 100 degrees out, I will bring a tailgating tent. This tent helps you from fainting in hot weather or keeps you and your food dry when it is raining. Do not let the weather stop you from having a great tailgating adventure, and just like road trips, take lots of pictures to remember when you are old and senile!

Melissa 'the Great'

About the Author

Melissa 'the Great' was born in upstate New York, but grew up in the south. She studied theatre and drinking at a very prominent University. She thanks her parents for her motto to live life to the fullest. She derives her comedy from observing herself through key moments in life and people watching. She calls herself Melissa 'the Great' because, well, she's great!

Go to www.tri-pub.com to get information about Triplicity Publishing or to submit your manuscript.

www.ingramcontent.com/pod-product-compliance
Lightning Source LLC
Chambersburg PA
CBHW060604030426
42337CB00019B/3596